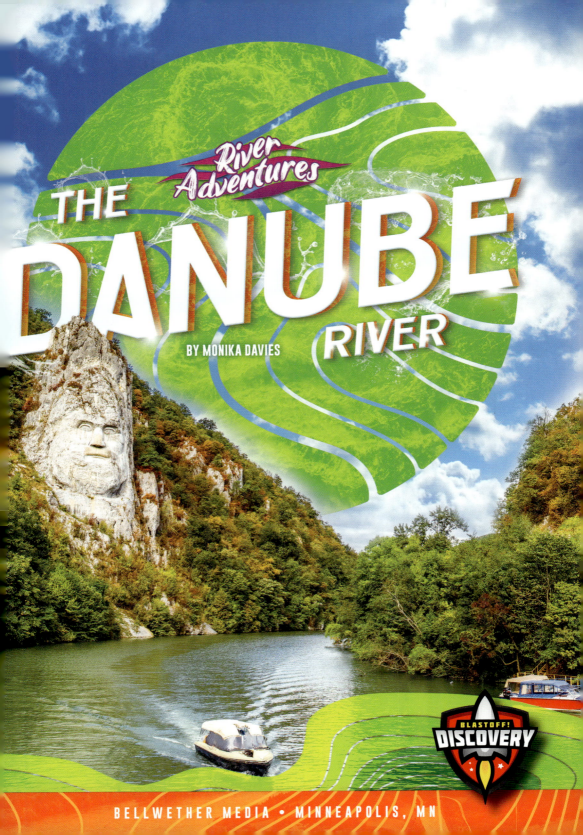

River Adventures

THE DANUBE RIVER

BY MONIKA DAVIES

BELLWETHER MEDIA • MINNEAPOLIS, MN

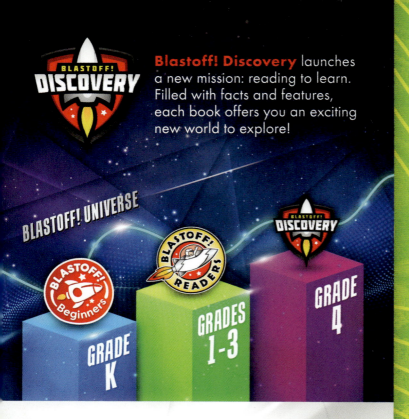

This edition first published in 2025 by Bellwether Media, Inc.

No part of this publication may be reproduced in whole or in part without written permission of the publisher. For information regarding permission, write to Bellwether Media, Inc., Attention: Permissions Department, 6012 Blue Circle Drive, Minnetonka, MN 55343.

Library of Congress Cataloging-in-Publication Data

Names: Davies, Monika, author.
Title: The Danube River / by Monika Davies.
Description: Minneapolis, MN : Bellwether Media, Inc., 2025. | Series: River adventures | Includes bibliographical references and index. | Audience: Ages 7-13 | Audience: Grades 4-6 | Summary: "Engaging images accompany information about the Danube River. The combination of high-interest subject matter and narrative text is intended for students in grades 3 through 8"– Provided by publisher.
Identifiers: LCCN 2024016560 (print) | LCCN 2024016561 (ebook) | ISBN 9798886879971 (library binding) | ISBN 9781644879290 (ebook)
Subjects: LCSH: Danube River–Juvenile literature. | Danube River Valley–Juvenile literature.
Classification: LCC DB446 .D38 2025 (print) | LCC DB446 (ebook) | DDC 949.6–dc23/eng/20240412
LC record available at https://lccn.loc.gov/2024016560
LC ebook record available at https://lccn.loc.gov/2024016561

Text copyright © 2025 by Bellwether Media, Inc. BLASTOFF! DISCOVERY and associated logos are trademarks and/or registered trademarks of Bellwether Media, Inc. Bellwether Media is a division of Chrysalis Education Group.

Editor: Rachael Barnes   Designer: Brittany McIntosh

Printed in the United States of America, North Mankato, MN.

TABLE OF CONTENTS

Cruising the Danube	4
Geography	6
Plants and Animals	12
Human History	16
The River Today	22
Protecting the River	26
Glossary	30
To Learn More	31
Index	32

CRUISING THE DANUBE

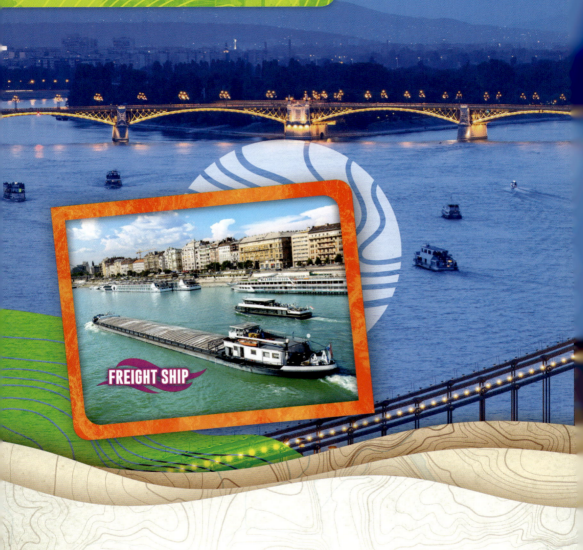

FREIGHT SHIP

A blanket of navy blue sky hangs over the Danube River. It is a crisp and starry summer night in Budapest, Hungary. **Tourists** board a ship to sightsee. They snap photos of buildings along the river. Their ship glides on the calm waters.

BUDAPEST, HUNGARY

A guide leads the tourists off the ship. The group strolls along the Danube **Promenade**. The guide points out **freight** ships as they sail past. Some ships will travel hundreds of miles to the river's **mouth** at the Black Sea!

GEOGRAPHY

At around 1,770 miles (2,849 kilometers) long, the Danube River is the second-longest river in Europe. It winds through 10 countries and flows mostly from west to east. The Danube starts its journey in Germany's Black Forest region. The river travels east across Germany. It flows through northern Austria and along Slovakia's southern border.

The river then turns south into the lowlands of Hungary. The Danube widens as it crosses Croatia and Serbia. It spreads out over **plains**. Its widest point is 4.3 miles (7 kilometers) across. The Danube flows slowly between Bulgaria and Romania. Finally, it touches Moldova before curving along Ukraine's southern border to stream into the Black Sea.

BICYCLING ALONG THE RIVER

The Danube Cycle Path spans from the Black Forest to the Black Sea. Most bikers travel a scenic riverside stretch that is about 746 miles (1,200 kilometers) long.

AUSTRIA

SAVA RIVER

TISZA RIVER

CONFLUENCE OF THE SAVA AND DANUBE RIVERS

Multiple bodies of water are connected to the Danube and contribute to the river's length. Over 300 **tributaries** add to the Danube as it flows across the continent. The Sava and Tisza are two major ones. The **confluences** of the two rivers and the Danube are near Belgrade, the capital of Serbia.

Other capital cities lie along the Danube. The river divides Budapest, Hungary. Austria's capital, Vienna, hustles and bustles next to the river. Bratislava, Slovakia, also straddles the Danube.

DANUBE DRAINAGE

The Danube River drains water from 19 countries. It drains around 315,000 square miles (815,846 square kilometers) of land!

BRATISLAVA

The Danube River can be divided into three parts. The upper section starts at the river's **source**. This is where two gentle streams, the Breg and Brigach, join together. The upper Danube cuts through mountain ranges, including the Austrian Alps. This section of the river then reaches the Hungarian Gates **gorge**.

DANUBE'S SOURCE

DJERDAP DEPTHS

The Danube River is deepest in Serbia's Djerdap Gorge. From the riverbed to the surface, the river is 295 feet (90 meters) deep!

DANUBE FORMATION

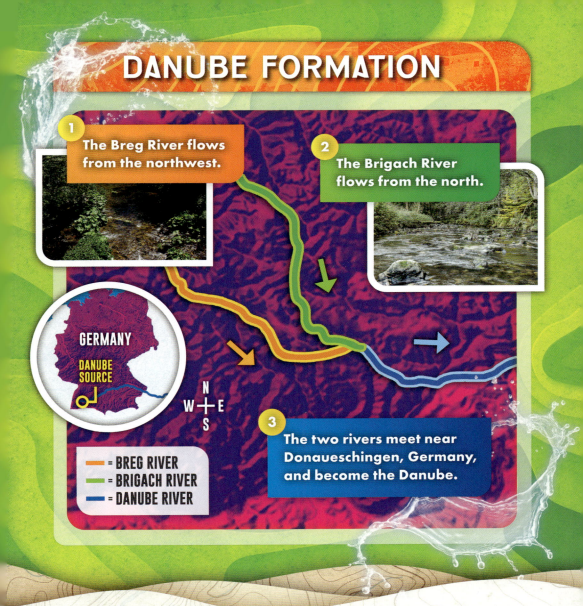

1. The Breg River flows from the northwest.
2. The Brigach River flows from the north.
3. The two rivers meet near Donaueschingen, Germany, and become the Danube.

GERMANY — DANUBE SOURCE

= BREG RIVER
= BRIGACH RIVER
= DANUBE RIVER

    The middle part of the Danube gushes from the Hungarian Gates to another gorge known as the Iron Gate. The lower Danube then flows toward the Danube **Delta**. The river splits into **channels** as it cuts through the huge **wetland**. These channels finally flow into the Black Sea.

PLANTS AND ANIMALS

There are a variety of **habitats** along the Danube. The river flows in fast streams down mountains. It is shallow and flows gently through lowlands. These habitats support thousands of plant and animal **species**.

Wildflowers grow on the river's banks. Red deer wander past poplar trees near the Alps. Beavers munch on the bark of alder trees. Kingfishers swoop over river reeds. Underwater, huge beluga sturgeons swim in the river. Salmon dip and dive in the cold water. Dice snakes hunt for fish on the river's floor.

RED DEER

BELUGA STURGEON

DANUBE SALMON

DICE SNAKE

COMMON KINGFISHER

EURASIAN BEAVER

Life Span: up to 25 years
Status: least concern

Eurasian beaver range = 🟩

| LEAST CONCERN | NEAR THREATENED | VULNERABLE | ENDANGERED | CRITICALLY ENDANGERED | EXTINCT IN THE WILD | EXTINCT |

The Danube Delta's mix of land and waterways is home to many species. Willow, linden, and oak trees grow on the land. A massive reed bed covers the wetland's lakes.

LOOK TO THE SKY

The Danube Delta is known as a bird-watcher's paradise. More than 300 species of birds fly over this landform.

DALMATIAN PELICAN

Life Span: up to 25 years
Status: near threatened

Dalmatian pelican range = 🟩

| LEAST CONCERN | NEAR THREATENED | VULNERABLE | ENDANGERED | CRITICALLY ENDANGERED | EXTINCT IN THE WILD | EXTINCT |

Pike and other fish swim in the Danube Delta. White-tailed eagles swoop down to hunt them. Dalmatian pelicans nest in banks of reeds. Frogs and toads call out from shallow waters. Wild cattle and wild horses graze on grasses. Carp and catfish swim through the streams.

15

HUMAN HISTORY

Castles and old **fortresses** stand tall next to the Danube River. They tell of the vast history of humans who relied on the river.

As early as 700 BCE, Greek sailors used the Danube as a trade route. Later, the river became the northern boundary of the Roman **Empire**. Roman **settlements** were established along the river. These settlements would later become a line of defense for the Ottoman Empire. Fortresses along the Danube protected the Empire in the 1400s CE.

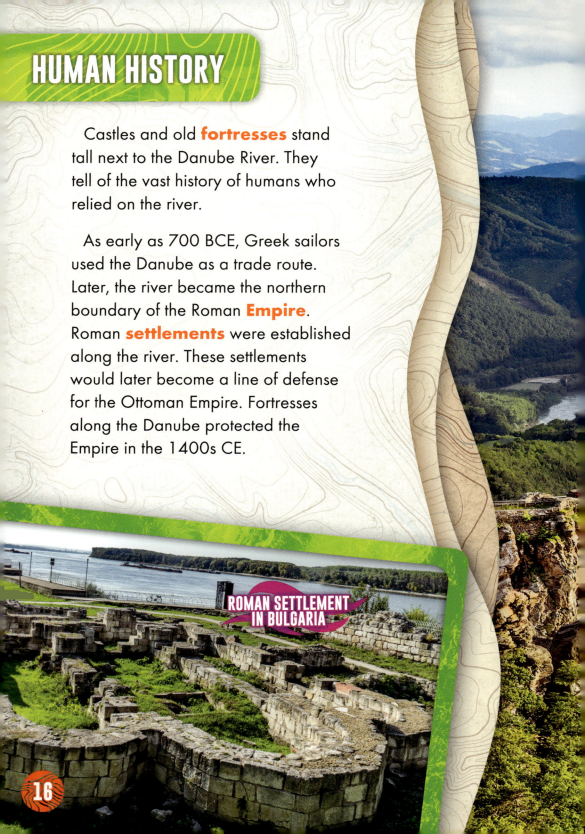

ROMAN SETTLEMENT IN BULGARIA

The former Roman settlements grew into Vienna, Budapest, Belgrade, and other cities. Nations continued to use the Danube as a defense until the 1800s.

BUDAPEST IN THE 1800s

PRESENT-DAY VIENNA

CULTURAL CONNECTION
THE BLUE DANUBE

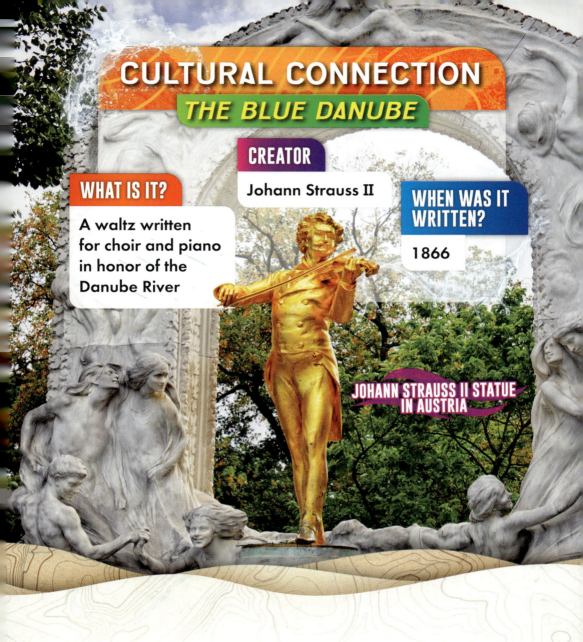

WHAT IS IT?
A waltz written for choir and piano in honor of the Danube River

CREATOR
Johann Strauss II

WHEN WAS IT WRITTEN?
1866

JOHANN STRAUSS II STATUE IN AUSTRIA

In 1830, a riverboat traveled on the Danube from Vienna to Budapest. Experts think the riverboat was likely sent for trade purposes. This journey marked a shift in the use of the Danube. It was now seen as a way to connect the countries on the river. The Danube became a major trade route. Many countries grew their economy by trading along the river.

SIGNING THE TREATY OF PARIS OF 1856

Nations began signing **treaties** to set rules for peaceful travel along the river. An Austro-Turkish treaty in 1616 was one of the first. It gave Austrians the right to travel the middle and lower sections of the river.

The Treaty of Paris of 1856 was another a key agreement. This treaty made the Danube free to travel for all nations. It also set up the Danube Commission. The commission's goal was to maintain the river as an international route.

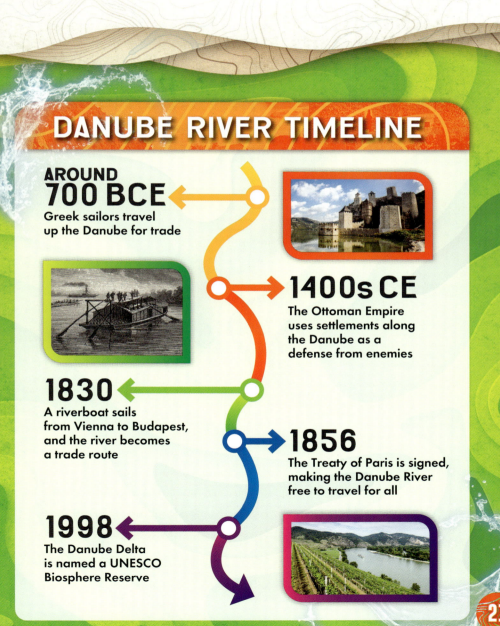

DANUBE RIVER TIMELINE

AROUND 700 BCE
Greek sailors travel up the Danube for trade

1400s CE
The Ottoman Empire uses settlements along the Danube as a defense from enemies

1830
A riverboat sails from Vienna to Budapest, and the river becomes a trade route

1856
The Treaty of Paris is signed, making the Danube River free to travel for all

1998
The Danube Delta is named a UNESCO Biosphere Reserve

THE RIVER TODAY

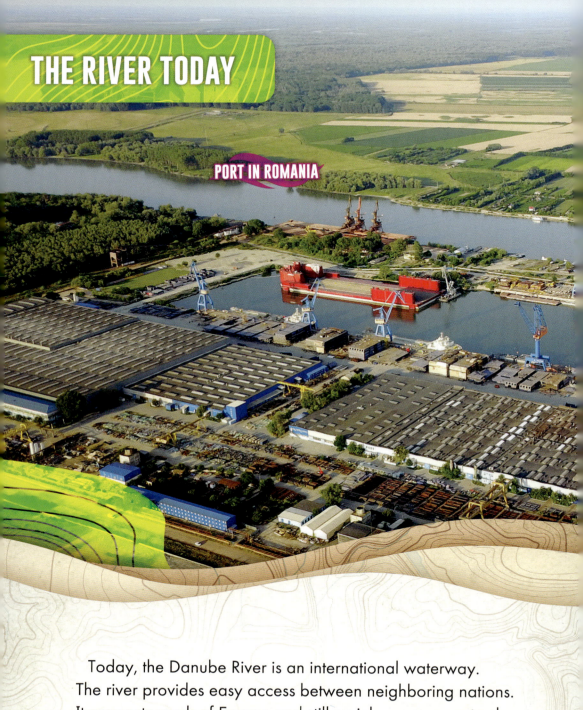

PORT IN ROMANIA

Today, the Danube River is an international waterway. The river provides easy access between neighboring nations. It connects much of Europe and still mainly serves as a trade route. Goods on ships are moved upstream and downstream. Many countries have ports where goods come and go.

ART MASTERS

The annual Danube Art Master contest encourages kids to explore and create art about the Danube! Kids can make art, videos, or maps to enter.

FISHING

TOURISM

Major cities grow and thrive next to the river. People love to bike, hike, camp, and fish along the Danube. Tourists travel to take in its beauty. The river often inspires people to make art!

MAIN-DANUBE CANAL

Human activity has changed the shape of the Danube. Important **canals** were built over the years. These canals help ships make their way through tricky sections of the river. The Main-Danube Canal in southern Germany is the longest.

Humans have also built **hydropower** dams along the Danube. These dams generate power from the river's running water. This form of power is important for nearly all countries that have access to the Danube. One of the largest dam systems on the Danube is in Gabčíkovo, Slovakia.

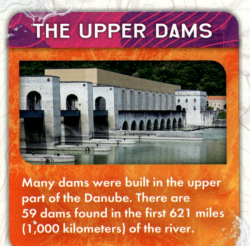

THE UPPER DAMS

Many dams were built in the upper part of the Danube. There are 59 dams found in the first 621 miles (1,000 kilometers) of the river.

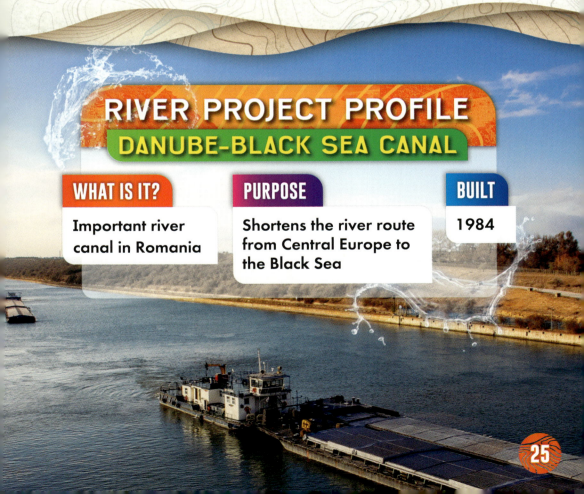

RIVER PROJECT PROFILE
DANUBE-BLACK SEA CANAL

WHAT IS IT?
Important river canal in Romania

PURPOSE
Shortens the river route from Central Europe to the Black Sea

BUILT
1984

PROTECTING THE RIVER

The Danube River lies at the heart of many countries. It supports many plants and animals. But frequent use threatens the health of the river. Humans are polluting the Danube. More plastic waste is found in the waters each year. **Chemicals** from nearby farms run into the river. Animals and plants living in the water cannot survive.

Hydropower dams change the path of the Danube. Less water flows to the river's tributaries and delta. Over time, this destroys habitats. Dams also stop fish from traveling up and down the river to lay their eggs. Fewer fish hurts the food chain.

PLASTIC WASTE

LOW WATER LEVEL

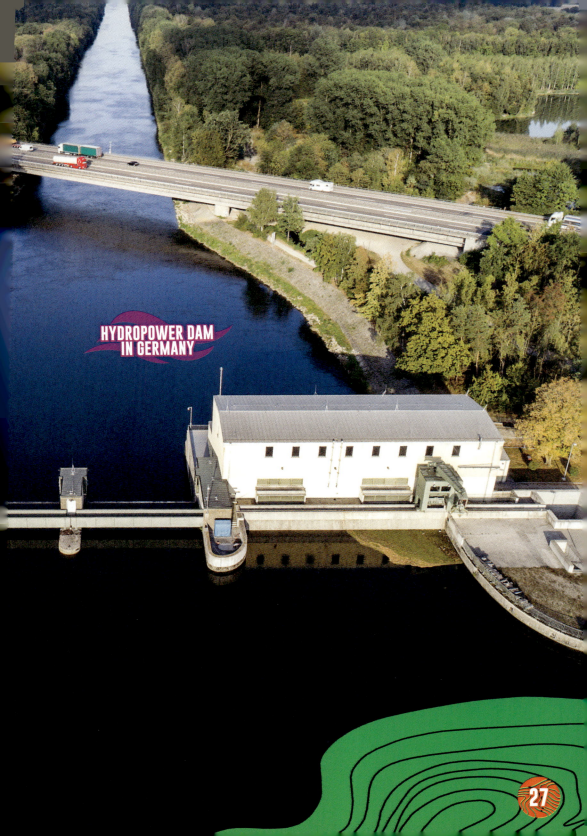

People are working to protect the Danube. The Danube River Protection Convention (DRPC) was created in 1994. A group of 11 countries agreed to help protect the Danube. Today, the DRPC and other groups monitor what is allowed in protected waters. Many wildlife organizations also track and research the health of the entire river.

People around the world can help by talking about the Danube! Sharing and discussing why the river is important encourages people to take care of the Danube. Humans can lend a hand to make sure the river remains full of life and beauty.

GLOSSARY

canals—human-made waterways that boats can travel through

channels—paths where water flows; channels often connect rivers to larger bodies of water.

chemicals—substances that are used to produce a change in another substance

confluences—places where two rivers meet

delta—a land area that forms where a river flows into a large body of water

empire—a group of people led by one ruler

fortresses—strong buildings used to protect soldiers and sometimes towns

freight—related to ships that carry goods

gorge—a narrow canyon with steep walls

habitats—lands with certain types of plants, animals, and weather

hydropower—related to the energy created by moving water

mouth—the place where a river empties into a larger body of water

plains—large areas of flat land

promenade—a public place where people often walk for fun and sightseeing

settlements—places that people move to and make their home

source—the beginning of a river

species—kinds of animals

tourists—people who travel to visit another place

treaties—official agreements between two groups

tributaries—rivers and streams that flow into a larger stream, river, or lake

wetland—an area of land that is covered with low levels of water for most of the year

TO LEARN MORE

AT THE LIBRARY

Coleman, Miriam. *The Geography of Europe*. New York, N.Y.: PowerKids Press, 2021.

Harris, Tim. *Wildlife Worlds Europe*. New York, N.Y.: Crabtree Publishing Company, 2020.

Miles, John C. *Pathways Through Europe*. New York, N.Y.: Crabtree Publishing Company, 2020.

ON THE WEB

FACTSURFER

Factsurfer.com gives you a safe, fun way to find more information.

1. Go to www.factsurfer.com.

2. Enter "Danube River" into the search box and click 🔍.

3. Select your book cover to see a list of related content.

INDEX

Austrian Alps, 10, 12
Belgrade, Serbia, 8, 18
Black Forest, 6, 7
Black Sea, 5, 6, 7, 11
Blue Danube, The, 19
Bratislava, Slovakia, 9
Breg, 10
Brigach, 10
Budapest, Hungary, 4, 5, 9, 18, 19
canals, 24, 25
confluences, 8
countries, 4, 5, 6, 7, 8, 9, 10, 16, 17, 18, 19, 20, 21, 22, 24, 25, 26, 27
cultural connection, 19
dams, 25, 26, 27
Danube Art Master, 23
Danube Commission, 21
Danube Cycle Path, 7
Danube Delta, 11, 14, 15, 26
Danube River Protection Convention, 28
Danube-Black Sea Canal, 25
Djerdap Gorge, 10
Europe, 6, 8, 22
formation, 11

history, 16, 18, 19, 20, 21, 24, 25, 28
Hungarian Gates, 10, 11
Iron Gate, 11
map, 6
mouth, 5
people, 4, 5, 7, 16, 20, 23, 24, 26, 28, 29
pollution, 26
ports, 22
river project profile, 25
riverboat, 19
Sava River, 8
sections, 10, 11, 20, 24, 25
ships, 4, 5, 22, 24
size, 6, 8, 9, 10
source, 10
timeline, 21
Tisza River, 8
tourists, 4, 5, 23
trade, 16, 19, 22
treaties, 20, 21
tributaries, 8, 10, 26
Vienna, Austria, 9, 18, 19
wildlife, 12, 13, 14, 15, 26, 28

The images in this book are reproduced through the courtesy of: Serenity-H, front cover; khunkornStudio, p. 3; givaga, p. 4 (freight ship); Boris Stroujko, pp. 4-5; Stefano Politi Markovina/ Alamy, pp. 6-7; Animaflora PicsStock, p. 7 (Danube Cycle Path); Miroslav Posavec, p. 8 (Sava River); Kurka Geza Corey, p. 8 (Tisza River); Bada1, p. 8 (confluence); Rasto SK, p. 9; mauritius images GmbH/ Alamy, p. 10 (top); BGStock72, p. 10 (bottom); JRG, p. 11 (left); Edgar G Biehle, p. 11 (right); WildMedia, p. 12 (kingfisher); Michael Eaton, p. 12 (red deer); Rostislav Stefanek, p. 12 (beluga sturgeon); benny337, p. 12 (Danube salmon); TAMER YILMAZ, p. 12 (dice snake); Wild Carpathians, p. 13; Vlad Vahnovan, p. 14 (top); bdavid32, p. 14 (bottom); Victor Maschek, p. 15; OmiStudio, p. 16; canadastock, pp. 16-17; De Luan/ Alamy, p. 18 (top); creativemarc, p. 18 (bottom); sun ok, p. 19; Édouard Dubufe/ Wikipedia, p. 20; Izabela Wierzbicka, p. 21 (Ottoman Empire settlement); Old Books Images/ Alamy, p. 21 (riverboat); Sergey Fedoskin, p. 21 (Danube Delta); Razvan25/ iStockphoto, pp. 22-23; Andrej Privizer, p. 23 (fishing); Calin Stan, p. 23 (tourism); blickwinkel/ Alamy, p. 24; Simlinger, p. 25 (top); Sebastian_Photography, p. 25 (bottom); sarenac77, p. 26 (plastic waste); SoneNS, p. 26 (low water level); Bim/ iStockphoto, pp. 26-27; Mita Stock Images, pp. 28-29; Sergey, p. 31.